Word Bird's™

Easter Words

Published in the United States of America by The Child's World®, Inc.
PO Box 326
Chanhassen, MN 55317-0326
800-599-READ
www.childsworld.com

Project Manager Mary Berendes
Editor Katherine Stevenson, Ph.D.
Designer Ian Butterworth

Library of Congress Cataloging-in-Publication Data
Moncure, Jane Belk.
Word Bird's Easter words / by Jane Belk Moncure.
p. cm.
Summary: Word Bird puts words about Easter in his word house.
ISBN 1-56766-626-4 (alk. paper)
1. Vocabulary—Juvenile literature. 2. Easter—Juvenile literature.
[1. Vocabulary. 2. Easter. 3. Holidays.] I. Title.
PE1449 .M5273 2001
428.1—dc21
00-010880

Word Bird's™

Easter Words

by Jane Belk Moncure

illustrated by Chris McEwan

Word Bird made a...

word house.

"I will put Easter words in my house," said Word Bird.

Word Bird put in these words:

butterfly

baby birds

new life

violets

daffodils

Easter lilies

tulips

Easter flowers

chicks

bunnies

ducklings

Easter animals

Easter Bunny

Easter eggs

jellybeans

chocolate egg

Easter candy

marshmallow chicks

chocolate bunnies

Easter-egg tree

Easter puppets

The Easter Bunny

His rabbity ears go flippity-flop
As he fills *my* basket to the top
With Easter treats for Easter day,
Then he hippity-hops away.

Easter verse

bunny hop

Easter baskets

Easter-egg hunt

Happy Easter

Put the egg
in the basket.

Easter party

Easter clothes

Easter parade

Can you read these Easter

new life

ducklings

 Easter flowers

Easter Bunny

Easter lilies

Easter eggs

tulips

 Easter candy

Easter animals

chicks

jellybeans

30

words with Word Bird?

Easter-egg tree

Easter-egg hunt

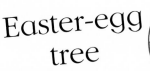 Easter puppets

 Easter party

Easter verse

His rabbity ears go flippity-flop
As he fills my basket to the top
With Easter treats for Easter day,
Then he hippity-hops away.

 bunny hop

Easter clothes

Easter baskets

Easter parade

You can make an Easter word house. You can put Word Bird's words in your house and read them, too.

Can you think of other Easter words to put in your word house?